Continued on page ii

D1042561

Inviting Silence

Inviting Silence

UNIVERSAL PRINCIPLES

OF MEDITATION

Gunilla Norris

BlueBridge

Cover design by Amy C. King
Cover photography by Getty Images
Text design by Jennifer Ann Daddio

Parts of this book were first published as *Sharing Silence*.

Library of Congress Cataloging-in-Publication Data

Norris, Gunilla Brodde, 1939-
Inviting silence : universal principles of meditation/
Gunilla Norris.—1st ed.
p. cm.
ISBN 0-9742405-0-8
I. Meditation. 2. Silence--Religious aspects. I. Title.
BL627.N658 2004
204'.35--dc22
2004015924

Published by
B L U E B R I D G E
An imprint of United Tribes Media Inc.
240 West 35th Street, Suite 500
New York, NY 10001

www.bluebridgebooks.com

Printed in the United States of America

3 5 7 9 10 8 6 4

Contents

This book is dedicated to all the

WONDERFUL PEOPLE

who have participated with me

over the years in meditation groups

and to my friend,

GRETA SIBLEY,

who produced the very first version

of this manuscript.

Introduction

People often contact me because they have lost some kind of meaning thread in their lives. Without a sense of meaning our lives lose their luster. We endure our days rather than embrace the living of them. To enter the realm of meaning requires attention and dedication. It requires an interior, reflective life. It requires the calming of our usual chattering minds. It requires trusting the life-giving nourishment of silence, that vast field of permission and sustenance in which our lives are held.

But we must want to dwell in that nourishment and to seek it consciously to have it. Fortunately, today we can learn ways to meditate from many different traditions. We can come to silence by practicing one of several Buddhist paths, or through Christian contemplative prayer, as well as through Jewish, Sufi, and Taoist disciplines. Traditions to quiet the mind and center the heart have most often been in the domain of religion. Spirituality, however, belongs to each one of us, no matter what our ethnic, cultural, or professional background might be. Whichever path brings us to practice, at the center there is silence— perennial, universal, inclusive, and radiant. Our true peace and home.

Throughout the years I have found that beneath whatever we might *think* our discontent is, we very much need three things: an awareness of our inner longing . . . the courage to act on behalf of that longing . . . and a sense of community to support and maintain our interior journey.

I like to think of this book as an invitation, hence the title, *Inviting Silence.* It is broken into four sections. The first, *Beginning Silence,* reflects on the understanding that longing and discontent is a wake-up call, an invitation to begin to begin. The second, *Growing Silence,* dwells on yearning itself as a path and the acceptance of ambivalence, which inevitably accompanies any deep change. Yearning has a way of making us more willing to start a personal meditation practice, and it illuminates the need to make conscious choices in daily life to support such a commitment. The third, *Practicing Silence,* describes the practice of meditation. It assumes that one has made a conscious choice to meditate on a regular basis. The fourth, *Sharing Silence,* encourages the idea of formal practice with others in order to deepen and sustain the experience of cultivating a peaceful heart.

This book is for individuals and spiritual friends to use alone or with each other. It is a simple guideline for anyone of any tradition, and is offered with reverence for all who honor and use silence as a way.

∞

Nothing in all creation

is so like God

as silence.

MEISTER ECKHART

I

Beginning Silence

Within each of us there is a silence
—a silence as vast as the universe.
We are afraid of it . . . and we long for it.

When we experience that silence, we remember
who we are: creatures of the stars, created
from the birth of galaxies, created
from the cooling of this planet, created
from dust and gas, created
from the elements, created
from time and space . . . created
from silence.

Silence is the source of all that exists,
the unfathomable stillness where vibration began
—the first oscillation, the first word,
from which life emerged. Silence is our deepest nature,
our home, our common ground, our peace.

Silence reveals. Silence heals.
Silence is where God dwells.
We yearn to be there.

∞

Beginning to Begin

Can we recognize that now and then there comes
an inner sense, a fleeting thought, a little yearning
to live our lives differently?

We don't know what this means or what it requires.
We shake these notions off like a dog shakes off water
and go about our business.

But the longing continues.

Who has time, we ask? What is it anyway?
Reorganize to do what? Stop?
Do nothing? Be quiet?
What for?

Our practical selves only know how to perfect,
produce and perform.
This, at least, we can see as useful. This has results.
We want to believe in this way of perceiving.

For a little while it seems to give us
some sort of self-image.

But the longing doesn't let us alone. It won't go away.
We become even busier perhaps
to "take care of it."
We numb ourselves with distractions—things to do,
consume, and maintain—
things to collect, experience, and entertain.
We can always think of more miles to run.

Still the little yearning continues. . . .

Could we sense that this longing is not lack
or something worse
—some kind of fundamental fault in us?
Could we receive it as an invitation instead,
a calling, a small voice inviting us home,
back to our truer self?

This shift in thought can move mountains.

It can let us begin to begin.

As Yearning Grows

Our efforts to make things "come out right"
and to have our lives "be meaningful"
according to our private notions and demands
doesn't quite do it.
Even when we are outwardly successful
in ways that our society rewards
something still seems to be missing.
We are at an impasse.

This is good to know and essential to feel.
Here we can discover that more pushing and striving
go nowhere. We start to slow down
with no solution for that persistent, nagging inner sense
that can be kept at bay but does not go away.
We are beginning to come to silence
and it is often uncomfortable at the start.

Slowly we discover that we are trying to have what we *do*
verify who we *are*. It always fails.

The effort is exhausting and finally empty.
Who we *are* is given to us. We do not ever earn it.
It is a free and holy gift.

The paradox is that we must stop, feel,
and grow silent
in order to receive the gift of ourselves
even while we still hang on to the belief
that things are all up to us,
that we are in charge.

We begin to intuit that effort has to be made
in a different way.
That is why the first experiences of silence
are often so frustrating and opaque.
We feel restless.
Somewhere inside us a treadmill grinds on.
We are neither here nor there. The gears do not mesh.
Deep down we know there is more.

What to do?

What to do?

Effort how?

When we apply a little pressure of the will

to listen to our longing

it becomes our friend. We are in fact yearning

for our essence, our true self.

This longing can be trusted if we do not avoid it

or dissipate it with increased doing

or patterns of distraction and consumption.

Over time as the inner pressure builds

we can inexplicably discover

that restlessness has become something

approaching willingness.

It is bringing us to the threshold of change.

It is asking us to take a first step.

Learning to Pause

In almost all traditions of spiritual development
there is the understanding that our wills
need to be trained. Without willingness
we cannot enter into stability
on behalf of our inner lives.

Willingness is not willpower,
the—"pull up your boot straps"—kind.
Willingness is more like surrender
to one's deep longing.
It orients us according to the heart's desire
instead of the ego's demands.

This requires recollection. A little space of time
to remember. Thoreau called it living
with a wide margin.
We can start by giving ourselves
just a tiny, small margin.

———

Without it being any more than simply stopping
we can pause all through the day to feel
ourselves in time and space.
This allows us to be located.

These little stops bring something of ourselves
back to the whole
the way a bee brings nectar to its hive.

When we learn to do this many times a day—
before getting out of bed, before meals,
before leaving for work,
before turning on a light or shutting it—
the pauses add up.

We are expressing a little pressure of the will.
Over time the habit of recollection leads us
back to the center,
to stillness and listening.

There we can begin to find

a new center from which to live.

The Found Treasure of Time

With more awareness we may discover
that small gaps in our daily round
can be places of silence. These are the found times
or rather the moments in which *we* ourselves are found.

Mostly they come when we are waiting:
in the doctor's office, on the telephone,
in traffic jams and the checkout line.

In just those moments we have an opportunity
to turn our attention to our physical being,
to the rhythm of our breath,
to the texture and feel of things around us.

By noticing particulars we can also begin
to notice the space in which they are held . . .
the vastness that holds everything—
the great lap of silence.

———

These waiting moments in our daily round
can turn out to be treasures. We can allow them
to support us instead of distracting us
or blocking us.

Here in each day is a wealth of time
we can take advantage of. They are breath breaks.
If we learn to rest and renew in them
our lives will go from disconnection and haste
to breathtaking presence.

Disappointment

Expectation is the great enemy of early practice.
We have internal pictures of what we think
peace and spiritual attainment should be.
We want to be successful and feel good about ourselves.

If we do not have immediate and recognizable
progress we feel like quitting.
Here is where many of us give up.
We shut the door. We say,
What's the use? I don't see anything different.
This is not adding up to anything.
I don't feel any better, and I'm not able to do this.

We think we might as well forget it,
might as well go with the mind's dominance,
the culture's drive, our old familiar habits,
the lure of substitute pleasures.
At least these are familiar—

we might even talk ourselves into thinking

that *this is all there is, anyway.*

We close the inner door or it slams shut by itself.

Our standstill seems permanent.

We may be here for months and even years.

The heart's longing, however, is very powerful.

It hasn't shut down though we may appear to have.

In the hiatus it gathers muscle and strength.

Not unlike a wave near the shore

it heaves into our lives again and again

in small ways or with the full thunder

and crash of its claim.

Sometimes we are knocked over

and drenched by its power.

We are being recalled to pick ourselves up

to begin again . . . however humbly,

finding perhaps that our longing,

while appearing to have ended, has gathered more force,

an insistence that can no longer be denied.

Stopping and Starting

One of the hardest lessons of any inner journey
is to understand that our ideal sense
of how things should be and the actual experience
are miles apart.

To *be* with our being . . .
is the most simple, direct, truly human capacity,
and it is the most difficult to sustain.
In two minutes of sitting quietly
we will soon discover that our minds have gone off
by themselves with plans, fantasies, judgments,
hopes, fears, and what have you!
In nothing flat we have flown away
from our presence in the present.

To accept that we do this all the time
is to accept the process of stopping and starting
again and again.

———

When we take an actual trip

it is what happens as well.

We go a distance. Then we stop.

We travel another distance,

often not seeing and doing what we thought we would,

but meeting whatever comes our way instead.

This happens on the inner plane, too.

We think we are moving towards a recognizable peace

or natural stillness

and we discover we are in the noisiest city of all—

our mind.

Stop. Start. Start. Stop

and start again.

We will do only relatively well

even when we have been on our path for years.

The Deepening Wish

It may not be clear that in the midst of ambivalence
we have, in fact, begun.
Approaching and avoiding, we are still snailing forward
towards a peace we sense can be ours one day.

What are the signs?
Discouragement laced with hope.
Curiosity buried in dismissal.
The deep conviction that we are not capable
giving way to the deeper longing that knows
that we are, indeed, very capable.

This stew of feeling and thought is the sure sign
that we are ripe to start.
It is the muddy, messy invitation
telling us it is high time
for a mindfulness practice, one that will allow us
to catch up with our longing
the way the soul catches up with the body.

II

Growing Silence

∞

In our present culture
silence is something like an endangered species . . .
an endangered fundamental.
We need it badly.

Silence brings us back to basics, to our senses,
to our selves. It locates us. Without that return
we can go so far away from our true natures
that we end up, quite literally,
beside ourselves. We live blindly and act thoughtlessly.
We endanger the delicate balance which sustains
our lives, our communities, and our planet.

Can we remember our power as persons?

Can we remind ourselves and others

that, nurtured in silence, our awareness

can lead us back to integrity and meaning?

Each of us has and is a holy capability.

The First Step

It may take months for us to sense
that our longing has *already* taken the first small steps.

Can we begin to notice some of the signs?
How we pause before something beautiful?
How we grow inexplicably silent more of the time?
How our breath seeks deeper exhalation?
How we close our eyes and gaze inward
as if drawn to another realm?

Can we catch our softening eyes
when we watch our children at play,
when our pets are up to their antics,
when we hold the aging hands of our parents?

These moments are hints that tell us
there is something inside
that doesn't live on a schedule,

doesn't entirely define itself by accomplishing tasks
or by keeping things going!

This part of us trusts another dimension,
the central fact of being.
It *already* knows that simple presence is
where our hearts come to peace.

How strange that it takes so long
to be in touch with this . . .
the most obvious fact of our lives.

Cultivating a peaceful heart is the journey of a lifetime.
When this truth comes fully into awareness
we can join it—a conscious first step.

We can start *to be* with our being.

Strengthening the Will

How to develop an ability to be constant?
Many people begin with a high resolve only to find
they cannot sustain their intention.
Their spiritual practice is soon abandoned.
They are discouraged and may not try again
for months, even years.

If we can accept that wallowing in regret
or self-judgment slows the process more,
we have a chance.
We can learn to be silent with ourselves
about our failures
and simply pick up where we left off,
thus saving countless hours.

We must just begin again.
That is the key.

We can choose to do something small—
one simple thing each day for a week.
This will train the will.

Perhaps we will practice two minutes
of grateful silence before and even after a meal.
Perhaps after making the bed
we will dwell in a moment of restful awareness.
Perhaps we will open a window to the morning
and let our minds open as well.
Allowing the air to caress us
we might appreciate the sweet gift of sensation.

These mindful moments are random examples.
Each of us can make our own sustainable practice
out of such small moments and so
strengthen the will and come to spiritual aliveness.
With one small, constant effort
one day at a time, we can grow.

Making Choices

When we pause and do it frequently, we begin
to be more aware of what is around us
and within us.

How can something so apparently simple
lead to such profound changes?
Ordinary as it is, this is a mystery
and one of great depth.
In it we come to trust an instinct, the nudge
that tells us when something is not quite right.
We can become aware of being off
and that we have a choice in the matter.

When things are too noisy, for instance, we may now
turn off the radio. The relief
when unnecessary stimulation is removed is amazing.
As we listen to the body's wisdom and attend to it
we are approaching some comfort with silence.

———

More and more in every day we begin to be aware
when things are too much or too frequent:
amounts of food on our plate, appointments
in our day timer, talk on the telephone,
hours in front of the computer.
These can take us away from presence in the present.

Daily choice is what builds a spiritual existence.
Faith in our essential connection to life
happens not by thought and belief
but by practice and persistence.
Making choices is how we exercise that faith.

It is always possible to ask, *What's enough*
here and now?
Our automatic selves act without choice.
Our knowing selves are wise and selective.

We know that too much, in the end, is too little

and that enough is always enough.

Listening to Life

On the surface, making these small, discerned choices

doesn't seem to be so important.

We tend to want to skip the work of it all.

It can seem relentless to be aware so much of the time.

Yet these choices are the very

structure of our lives.

Just as the pine needle or the seed

an ant brings to its hill

is the stuff out of which the hill is constructed

so our choices can bring us peace

or continuing chaos.

Pausing often helps us remember

and value our ability to choose.

Doing so with awareness, remembering to ask

What's enough here and now?

takes us deeper. We will find ourselves

ripening into another way of being. It happens
as silently and as slowly as an apple turning red.

Asking the simple question:
What will serve life today?
is a penetrating practice.
Not what will serve *me, my problems, my family,*
my desires or worries.
Such questions only lead us to the realm of worry.
When we ask, *What will serve life right here and now?*
we begin to live in a larger picture.

Whatever circumstances we find ourselves in,
this question can help us focus our intentions.
It is so fundamental it should lie within
every small choice we make, not just the big ones.
What will serve life today?

———

Life does not mean our own small ego's insistence
on its own way. It means something else.
What will allow for the greatest good
in a particular, local setting . . .
keeping in mind ourselves, the people in our lives,
the environment, and the community?

Hearing our answer from deep within
and following its direction
will turn us slowly towards peace,
a peace we may not understand
but one that opens us to new meaning.

Support

It is hard to set aside a consistent time
for meditation whether together or alone.
To practice formally we need support.

We will want our families to understand
that we are making a commitment
and that we need the practice
the way a plant needs water.

To sit by ourselves is difficult.
It helps a lot if someone we care about knows
what we are doing. Perhaps they will agree to take care
of the inevitable interruptions during our silent time.
Perhaps they will remind us
when we have forgotten our practice
and encourage us to get to it. It is important
to ask for this support and understanding.

———

If we live alone we might ask a friend
to encourage us in our effort.
We take shape in each other's awareness.
Asking for support often deepens commitment.

It helps to decide how much time
we will sit each day. Such a boundary around
the vastness of silence makes it less difficult.
It's good to start small. Five minutes. Ten minutes.
Do-able minutes.

Each of us must construct the small ways
that will scaffold our silence.
In the end we must simply practice.
Experience builds experience.
We must just do it.

III

Practicing Silence

∞

We do not need to be experts or gurus or geniuses
to remember that all of existence is precious.
We do not need cathedrals to remind ourselves
to experience the sacred. We need only to be
deeply respectful of what is fundamentally true;
and that is what we rediscover
when we center ourselves in silence.

Each of us can make a difference.
Politicians and visionaries will not return us
to the sacredness of life.
That will be done by ordinary men and women

who together or alone can say,
"Remember to breathe, remember to feel,
remember to care,
let us do this for our children and ourselves
and our children's children.
Let us practice for life's sake."

Here are reminders of some essential attitudes
and principles which can be helpful
in any meditation practice.
They are offered with reverence for all who honor
and use silence as a way.

∞

Room

When we make a place for silence, we make room
for ourselves. This is simple. And it is radical.
A room set apart for silence becomes a sanctuary
—a place for breath, for refreshment, for challenge,
and for healing. It is helpful to keep the space plain
and simple: a few cushions, a rug . . .
Simplicity allows the senses to rest from stimulation.

Silent spaces invite us to go to the inner room
—the room inside ourselves.
By making room for silence, we resist
the forces of the world which tell us to live
an advertised life of surface appearances,
instead of a discovered life—a life lived in contact
with our senses, our feelings,
our deepest thoughts and values.

When a space is reserved
solely for mindfulness practice,

the silence seems to deepen. A room devoted to silence
honors and invites the unknown, the untamed,
the wild, the shy, the unfathomable
—that which rarely has a chance to surface
within us. It is a visible,
external symbol of an internal reality:
an actual room
signifying space within ourselves
set aside for silence.

Preparation

Before we eat a meal, we purchase food and prepare it.
Before we go on a journey, we assemble and pack
the things we need. Any activity requires preparation.
This is true for a time of silence as well.

We need a place to practice silence,
and we also need an atmosphere—a sense of harmony,
an ambiance of quiet beauty to help us on the way.

We can arrange a vase of flowers or simple greens
to soothe our eyes and help us recall
that we are part of nature, part of the order of things.

We can light a candle to ease our passage
into a different mode of being.
Perhaps it will remind us that we have inner light
to discover and share.

———

We can burn a stick of incense
to mark time, as Buddhist monks do:
a short stick for a half-hour of sitting,
a longer stick for forty-five minutes . . .
aromatic time. Odor reminds us
that we are sensate creatures,
that our souls live in and through our bodies.

We can strike a bell at the start of a period of sitting.
We can let the sound ring into us
—let it sound us, as in navigation, to find our depth.

Preparations like these help us to be more present
on the journey into our selves, into the world
we share in silence.

Presence

We cannot really experience anything without being
present to it. True presence requires that we be attentive
to what is happening here and now. It is an offering
of our awareness, our participation, and our willingness.
This is a basic and profound courtesy.
By such courtesy we are deeply transformed.

In silence we discover ourselves, our actual presence
to the life in us and around us. When we are present,
deeply attentive, we cannot be busy controlling.
Instead we become beholders—giving ourselves up
to the mystery of things. We become more willing
to let things be. And, as a consequence
we can also let ourselves be.

This is so simple . . . and so hard.
Many of us have become uncomfortable with silence.
We do not regard it as a friend. In its presence
we feel uneasy, out of control.

We seek superficial reassurance for our busy minds,
instead of the deep confidence offered
by our silent vitality.

It takes time to rediscover the treasure of silence.
In it we can be found again. But we learn this
only by learning. By being present, moment to moment,
we may discern the richness of silence in ourselves
and in each other.

Through silence our days are illumined—like rooms
filled with light—so we may inhabit our lives.

Posture

When we sit in mindfulness practice
our backs should be straight.
Our upright posture took millions of years
to evolve. This gives our bodies
an inherent dignity.

When we are upright in body we tend to be present
and alert in spirit as well. Energy can travel freely
along the spine, dancing up to the crown of the head
and down to the sacrum.

Crown and sacrum. These words hint at our worth.
When we hold ourselves with dignity we acknowledge
the royal and sacred nature of our true selves.

Practice

Walking, eating a meal, dancing, breathing, chanting—
anything can be a practice so long as we are mindful,
so long as we are fully present. There are many ways,
many traditions.

To bring silence into our bodies and minds,
we must learn to be quiet. We begin by being still.
If a period of physical stillness is all we can muster,
that is enough. We have begun to practice.

If we can simply learn to follow our breath
in a steady way—attending to the inhalation
and the exhalation until we feel that we are no longer
breathing, but are being breathed
—we have grown in practice.

The point of practice is not to perform,
but to participate—not to achieve specific experiences,
but to develop a new relationship to experience itself.

When we no longer need to know or be something
other than what we are, we are free.
We can then experience the pure unfolding of life,
the rapture of living. This makes happiness possible.

From the deep well of silence, joy is
constantly bubbling up and flowing out.
Practice reveals that we are immersed in that joy.
Practice also reveals what is blocking the flow.

Principles

A few basic principles are helpful
in any mindfulness practice.

The first is precise intention. By focusing
on one objective during a period of meditation,
we grow in concentration. We may choose to follow
our breath, note our body's sensations or track
the pattern of our thoughts. The objective itself
is not so important as staying with it.

The second principle is permission—allowing
whatever comes up in the mind
in relation to our chosen objective.
If we are open-hearted and permissive
to the internal flow of events,
the habitual ways in which we congeal
against experience will be broken down,
releasing us into new life.

———

The third principle is persistence.
In returning to the practice over and over,
whether we feel like it or not,
we gain in peacefulness—no matter what
kind of experience we are having.

The fourth principle is acceptance of the fact
that we cannot be perfect in our practice.
We can do what we can do.
We can be relatively still, relatively focused,
relatively allowing. Our capacity is different
in every period of silence. No matter what
our daily practice is like, however,
there is a perceivable gain over time.

If we are open to this process,
we may derive a deep sense of satisfaction
from the knowledge that we are participating
in something larger than ourselves.

Pace

Learning to be measured, to be steady in our pace,
is a process that must take place in the body.
When we strive to do things we are learning strife.
When we strain we are learning strain.
In time practice helps us learn to move more easily,
to be un-driven, to flow.

Study the way waves wash onto the shore,
or the way rings float out on a lake
when a pebble splashes through the surface,
moving without apparent effort. There is
an organic pace to this. We, too, have an organic pace.
Silence can help us feel it.

When we sit quietly we will sense
how long an interval of sitting is right for us.
When we practice steadily we will also know
how often to return to silence in any given day.

———

In our culture we do not trust time.
We try to defy time. We steal time. We kill time.
We want to control the flow of events,
instead of trusting in a natural progression—
instead of trusting that we can and will
meet life as it happens.

We attack life to defend against the mistrust
we have of ourselves. In silence we can learn
to change this. We can give ourselves time,
leaning into it, resting in it. When we do this
the pressure comes off
and we give ourselves permission to feel
and experience—we can participate
in our lives without having to control events.
Then like still ponds at early dawn
we reflect effortless effort.

Suffering

Through the practice of silence we become aware
of our pain. The pain is always there—in our minds
and in our bodies. Silence allows us to see it,
face it, release it.

We constantly judge ourselves.
Our minds decide
what our experience should be
or should not be
—relentlessly labeling things good or bad—
demanding that our lives conform to our labels.
Then, when pain comes into our lives
—and it does to every life—we do not only suffer it,
but we suffer our suffering as well.
We add the mind's harsh judgment of pain
to our actual experience of it.

By practicing silence, we may discover the ways
in which we intensify our pain by judging it.

Then we have a chance to become less harsh,
more forgiving.

The pain created by our minds is stored in our bodies,
creating rigid patterns of behavior, blocking the flow
of energy within us, cramping our being.
Our harshness and our fears are embodied in our flesh.

In silence, we can feel these tendencies to congeal—
and allow them to be as they are. They may then
uncramp and release, for anything that is not resisted
tends of its own accord to unfold and change.

By cultivating silence, we can find and release
deeper and deeper levels of pain and so discover
once again what is beneath the pain:
the natural joy that is already inside us,
free to rise and flow into expression.

Predisposition

The fears in our unconscious minds create
particular ways of defending against full participation
in our lives. For whatever reason, we are
each predisposed to act and respond in certain ways.

By looking closely at these patterns as we sit,
we may learn a great deal about ourselves.
Perhaps we will encounter chronic sleepiness,
discovering that we lack the energy to remain awake
and attentive. Looking deeply we might find
that in our childhood we did not receive enough
attention, enough engagement, and learned to sleep
through the pain of neglect. In silence we may
slowly learn to value and participate with ourselves.

We may find that we are measuring ourselves
against others, comparing and monitoring. Looking
deeply into our childhood, we might discover
that we were asked to perform,

instead of being enjoyed.

Perhaps we never had a chance to know

the pleasurable people we are. In silence

we can let go and feel our incomparable selves.

We may feel chronic anger rising up, a hot gall.

Perhaps we were not fully heard when we were young.

We may have been shamed, or treated unjustly.

Our natural rhythms of behavior, self-discovery, or

expression may have been broken in some way,

leaving a residue of frustration in our bodies.

In silence we can learn to hear our forgotten selves,

to feel and to respond to the deep levels of our identity

that are surfacing at last.

We may discover a tremendous greed, old feelings

of having been cheated, overlooked, and dismissed.

We may actually feel the automatic impulses, which are

the beginnings of our compensation for such feelings

—the compulsions that lead to over-eating,
over-working, drinking, excessive sexual activity.
These compensations are meant to soothe,
to remind ourselves that we exist, but ultimately
they hurt us. In silence we can learn much about this.

We may come to realize that our habitual doubt
is a mask for self-deprecation—an unwillingness
to acknowledge what we have and what we are.
We may find that our boredom is simple laziness
—a refusal to pay attention. We may see
that our discouragement is based on false ideas
of entitlement. We think we are owed when we are not.
The lessons of silence are myriad.

In silence we have the common goal to honor
and protect our spirits. We are not being diagnostic
or prescriptive with one another. We are making
profound room in ourselves—for ourselves and

for each other. Then our inner habits can come up as they will, one by one, and we can smile at them. We can suffer them directly. We can slowly learn to accept what cannot be changed . . . and what is already whole and good within us.

Paradox

It is a paradox that we encounter so much internal noise
when we first try to sit in silence.

It is a paradox that experiencing pain releases pain.

It is a paradox that keeping still can lead us
so fully into life and being.

Our minds do not like paradoxes.
We want things to be clear,
so we can maintain our illusions of safety.
Certainty breeds tremendous smugness.

We each possess a deeper level of being, however,
which loves paradox. It knows
that summer is already growing
like a seed in the depth of winter. It knows
that the moment we are born, we begin to die. It knows
that all of life shimmers, in shades of becoming

—that shadow and light are always together,
the visible mingled with the invisible.

When we sit in stillness we are profoundly active.
Keeping silent, we can hear the roar of existence.
Through our willingness to be the one we are,
we become one with everything.

Steadfastness

How do we sustain the courage
and the will to continue our practice
when the going gets rough?
We know it will get rough,
and that we will encounter weariness,
frustration, and doubt.

Practicing mindfulness is much like physical training.
The long-distance runner must deal with hills
as well as valleys. The hills are hard.
And they make one strong.
If we can welcome them, and know
that they will be followed by valleys,
we will be learning something about steadfastness.

We may find the strength to continue
by taking the long view: recognizing
that bliss and pain are part of each other,
that both together are more than either is separately.

Together they form reality,
the only thing that truly satisfies us.

Alternatively we may look closely enough to see
that perseverance is also a matter of valuing
what is happening now—for its own sake.
Moment to moment, we continue by engaging fully
in the rich, dense, prolific dance of life.

Taking the long view and looking closely . . .
background and foreground,
by perseverance—through perseverance—
we become steadfast and sturdy.
We become present.

Phenomena

As we sit we may experience many different sensations:
our bodies may become very warm or very cold,
our skin may become prickly and uncomfortable.
There may be a melting feeling, as if liquid gold
was coursing through us. We may see beautiful colors,
smell unusual odors. We may hear the body/mind
get stuck in old conversations,
or repeating tunes from the hit parade.

These phenomena are not of much importance.
They are not to be hungered after
or assiduously avoided. They just happen
as the body and mind begin to release
the congealed tensions of experience.

Any phenomenon may be selected
as an object of concentration.
When one becomes especially dominant,
we have little choice but to make it our focus.

As we do this, we may discover that the phenomena
we find so compelling are not static.
They are continually changing, moving, and passing
on to something else.

Bit by bit, we may learn to see that everything
is impermanent, always rising or falling. We may learn
that all phenomena rest on something deeper;
something vast, endless and timeless—our source.

Particularity

We are not static beings, and yet we are called to be
exactly who we are. Our specific genetic code,
our parental influence, our education, our friends,
our work, our whole history of experiences
—these are all the particulars through which
we have become who we are now.

When we truly acknowledge
and embrace these particulars
we are making a profound contribution.
We are consciously accepting our limits,
even as they continue to change.
This is both solemn and joyful. It is what we,
as conscious beings, are asked to do—to accept
our small and unique places in this universe.

Just as water is the natural element of a fish,
our element is the vastness of life;

a fish can know water only living in it,
swimming in it and drawing it in through its gills.

A fish cannot know water except as a fish.
So, too, with us. We can know our true place,
our purpose, and our source only through our humanity
—by experiencing the vastness that is moving
through our small particularity.
Then we will feel intimately known,
trusted and upheld.

Passion

Because passion is an expression of love,
it encompasses suffering as well.
Love and suffering are always intertwined.

When we suffer what is truly ours to suffer, we move
into union with ourselves. We want this experience
of love, and we are afraid of it.

On some level, we know that the true meaning
of suffering is found in allowing each moment to be
what it is, remaining open to the vastness
—the life—
that wants to move through us.
Where, but in silence, can we be present enough
to witness that urge of life within?

We discover these depths through silence, stillness
and the simple act of being attentive with others.
As we enter into exquisite awareness of the life

that wants to live *as us,* we learn to love deeply.

We claim our passion.

IV

Sharing Silence

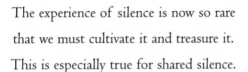

The experience of silence is now so rare
that we must cultivate it and treasure it.
This is especially true for shared silence.

To come together in silence
—even just a very few people—
creates a field of consciousness,
an awareness force.
This power helps us to see
our lives more truly.
Each of us can make a tremendous difference
simply through our intent and constancy.

In this way sharing silence is, in fact,
a political act. When we can stand aside from the usual
and perceive the fundamental, change begins to happen.
Our lives align with deeper values
and the lives of others are touched and influenced.

We can ask others to practice with us.
Together we can grow and make a difference.
Sharing silence with others is a profound act of trust,
love, and courtesy. It is a mutual gift, a necessity,
a helping hand, a path, and a discipline.

∞

Relationship

To become ourselves we need others.
Only in and through relationship do we truly become
persons. We know this from childhood.
We first learn of our existence through the eyes
of our parents. They are our first mirrors.

The process of learning who we are
—and who we might become—continues
through all the relationships of our lives.
In the deep resonance of companionship
we dare to journey to the center.

It is important to recognize how much we need
each other. This recognition removes the illusion
that we are self-created. It teaches us that giving
and taking are like inhaling and exhaling
—the breath of relationship.

———

By recognizing our need for each other we acknowledge
that every aspect of reality is connected to the whole,
that nothing is separate from us.

Sharing silence with others creates a bond
that cannot be compared to ordinary exchanges.
It helps us know that each of us is essential:
a vibrating essence. We can sense that vibration.
We can feel it singing in our cells.

When we speak, when we act, when we offer each other
food and water, we give form and expression
to the essential vibration within us. We become,
in a sense, living words. Words in combination
make complete, meaningful phrases.
Through this collaboration, potentials can be realized.
Worlds are created. In the language of life,
we are words of power.

———

When we support the silence in one another,
we discover what we each have been given to be.

The silence in each of us is the medium
through which the words we are may be spoken,
clearly and purely. In silence we are revealed.
This is universal and very personal.

Basics

The basic procedures for a period of shared meditation
are wonderfully simple:

Select a peaceful, undisturbed room.
Bring in some cushions and chairs to sit on.
Settle down and allow stillness to happen.

Each period of sitting may last from thirty minutes
to an hour or more.
A single period of perhaps forty-five minutes,
once a week, is a good first goal—
though a group may wish to begin
with thirty minutes until everyone can sit
comfortably for longer periods.

A bell is rung to signify the start of silence
and the beginning of meditation.
With informal groups outside of a specific tradition
or prescribed methodology,

how we sit is a private matter.
Some of us close our eyes;
some keep them open but unfocused.
Sitting cross-legged
with a straight back is recommended,
but some of us cannot do this
and prefer to sit with back support, legs outstretched.
Others may choose to use a kneeling bench or a chair.

After some designated time, with some allowance
for an intuitive sense of the right moment,
the bell is rung again to end a sitting period.

How can something so seemingly basic and simple
be the means for us to touch our center?
No one can tell us. We must simply do it,
not just once, but over and over again.
Though we sit together we must each sit alone—

it is also how we live life.

Alone, together. Together, alone.

Punctuality

A group that sits needs a time to begin
—and everyone must agree to be on time.
Starting a period of silence
and having it broken by someone's late arrival
is like the shattering of a glass.
The silence must be recovered bit by bit
and then reassembled. This takes time and effort,
and everyone must do it—not just the one who was late.

It is not so easy to be punctual, but it is important.
The discipline of punctuality is a self-courtesy.
It teaches us to value ourselves, each other,
and the time we have been given.

To be on time we need to experience ourselves in time.
Our inner lives are timeless,
and yet our days are numbered.
To work with time we need a sense of leisure,

a sense of the natural unfolding of a day,

of a season, a year, a life.

We need also to be present to our experiences,

moment to moment. This makes for timeliness.

Then we can feel the rhythm of our lives.

Our timing becomes finer and finer.

We do not miss a beat. Leisurely and precise,

we can flow with time.

Mutuality

When we form a group to practice silence
it is helpful to share the leadership.
It allows everyone to feel that it is *his or her* group.
If only one person leads, others may become lazy,
resentful or bored. By taking turns, we acknowledge
that all of us make up the whole.
Our responsibility is mutual. We all respond
(which originally meant to "pledge back")
by giving and receiving equitably.

When we form a group for sharing silence,
commitment to it is essential.
Our promise to each other is that we will be present
to ourselves and therefore to one another.
Together we make a holding place, much like the stones
in a well: side by side, they make a containment
for the living water to rise through the ground,
so that anyone can draw from it.

———

There is no well if the stones are not steady.

As in all deep things, constancy is necessary.

Through it we become sturdy, reliable, and trustworthy,

and so find our ground water.

Mutuality and commitment—in life as in sitting,

we must give of ourselves in order to receive.

Inspiration

It can be helpful to have a focus
to begin a period of silence.
Subjects can be selected that are universal and essential,
such as *trust, simplicity, compassion,* or *community.*
To begin a period of sitting the day's leader may speak
from personal insight and experience
or may read to the group
something carefully chosen from a book.

One might ask: Why read or speak at all
if the point is to be together in silence?
An answer might be that words can both grow
out of silence and bring us to it.
We can be inspired to go deeper.

The discursive, conceptual mind is always at work.
By giving it something to work with
we allow our non-conceptual mind
—the *being* part of us—

to sink deep into the well of silence
and breathe the mystery of what always is
and can never be named.

A lovely added benefit of shared leadership is
that the qualities of each participant in the group
begin to be known over time.
We are always ourselves,
whether we speak or are silent. Our essence is
revealed and refined in the practice of silence.
It is that living, luminous core
which in the end is the greatest gift
we can give to one another.
It is true inspiration . . . the breathing of life.

Dedication

In many spiritual traditions

there is a practice of dedicating any act

of devotion to something beyond ourselves.

This happens in the secular world as well.

We walk, run or swim for causes

as well as collect donations for them.

To be in solidarity with suffering

is a natural outgrowth of practicing silence.

The more we still ourselves, the more we become aware

of the huge context we are in

and the more we cannot ignore the suffering around us.

We are in this world,

and inextricably connected to every part of it.

We are exquisitely vulnerable—every one of us.

We know at every moment there is nothing

fixed or solid to stop the flow of life.

To be in deep equanimity in such flux and change

is what cultivating silence can teach us.

It brings us to the heart of things.

Millions of people have found support

in knowing that others are sitting *for them*,

and have for years without number.

The great teachers have shown us that peace is possible.

They dedicated their practice to seekers like us.

In a small way we can do the same.

Every period of silence can mindfully be dedicated

to the suffering and beauty of aspects of our world.

We can donate our thoughts, our goodwill and

our money to causes that pull on our hearts.

We can dedicate our work to the big work

—the shared gift of peace.

Continuity

When a sitting group remains stable
through months and years,
deep communion and trust grow,
along with the capacity to dwell in silence
for longer and longer periods of time.

Meditation is greatly enriched
by the discipline of sustained concentration
—a whole day, a week, even a month.

We can be afraid or unable to leave our daily round
to practice in this intense way,
yet the rewards are great.
It is not uncommon that our inner longing
not only draws us there,
but gives us the strength to manage
longer periods of sitting.

———

In the end, what really matters is continuity.

A path is not a path without it.

When we find our chosen way we must keep to it.

In doing so we will be fundamentally changed,

and we will find ourselves participating in a peace

that lies beyond understanding.

Peace

Peace is not absence of strife.
Peace is acceptance
and surrender to that which is.
Peace is the profound awareness of
the one true source
from which all things emerge . . .
and to which all things return.

However lost we may feel,
we are never outside of the source.
We are intimately known by it,
sustained by it, and returned to it
—daily . . . now . . . and when we pass away.
The source delights in us,
becomes in us, plays in us.

When we contact the source,
our practice has led us to the end
and to the beginning.

Then we can be at peace
—for no matter what occurs in our lives,
we can always find our way home
to the core, the truth of our being.

Silence is the friend

that never betrays.

CONFUCIUS